Better Homes and Gardens®

CREEPY MONSTERS

Hi! My name is Max. I have some great projects to show you—and they're all about monsters! We're going to have lots of fun making them together.

Inside You'll Find...

Practice a sequencing activity that teaches the correct order of events.

Kooky Creatures

The sun is just waking up and so are Max and his friends. Soon they'll be busy getting ready for school. What's the first thing you do in the morning when you wake up?

What happens first and last?

Look at the first two pictures of Max, below. What would you do first? Put the bread in the toaster? Or, spread the toast with jam? Look at the next two sets of pictures and decide which picture would come first in each set.

Remodel a fast-food sandwich container into a toy monster.

Ugfuzz

Can you guess why this monster is called an Ugfuzz? It's because he's a little bit ugly and a little bit fuzzy. And look at that B I G mouth! Do you think he'll try to gobble you up?

What you'll need...

- 1 small plastic-foam box
- White crafts glue
- Dryer lint (see Fuzzy Facts on page 7)
- Construction paper
- Scissors
- Tape
- Pencil
- 1 bendable plastic drinking straw

1 Use the front of the box, where it opens, as the mouth. To make the fur, spread some glue over part of the box. Firmly press a piece of dryer lint into the glue (see photo). Keep gluing dryer lint onto the sides and top of the box until it is covered.

2 Use construction paper to cut out eyes and teeth for the monster. Tape the eyes and teeth to the box (see photo).

3 With adult help, use a pencil to punch a hole near the center of the bottom of the box. Push the bendable end of the straw partway through the hole. Bend the straw and tape it to the inside of the top of the box (see photo).

Push up on the straw to make the monster's mouth open.

Fuzzy Facts

Many kinds of monsters have fuzzy, furry bodies. Besides dryer lint, you can use any of these fuzzy ideas to dress your monster: cotton balls, pipe cleaners, strips of ribbon, tissue paper, pom-poms, polyester fiberfill, and fabric strips.

Paint a picture with a sponge—it's especially easy for younger artists.

The Blob

A blob can be any size, shape, or color. It can be silly or scary. That's what makes it fun. It's anything you want it to be.

What you'll need...

- Newspaper or brown kraft paper
- 2 pieces of construction paper
- Scissors
- Tape (optional)
- Tempera paint
- 1 disposable tray or dish
- 1 damp sponge or a crumpled-up piece of plastic wrap
- Crayons or markers

1 Cover your work surface with newspaper. To make a pattern for The Blob, draw a shape on 1 piece of paper. Cut or tear out the shape (see photo).

Place The Blob pattern on top of the remaining piece of paper. If desired, use tape to hold the pattern and the piece of paper together.

2 Pour a little paint into the tray. Dip one end of the sponge into the paint. Hold the pattern steady with one hand. Dab the sponge along the edges where the pattern and piece of paper meet (see photo).

Remove the pattern. If you like, move the pattern to another part of the paper and repeat the painting step.

3 Let the paint dry completely. If you like, save the pattern for another picture.

Use crayons to draw a face on your Blob any way you like (see photo).

Mostly Ghosts

"Th . . . th . . . there are ghosts in there," said Elliot, shivering.
"Are you sure?" asked Max. "I don't see anything."
Can you find the 10 ghosts and 5 goblins that are hiding?

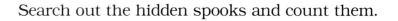

Host a ghost party and let the kids design their costumes.

Glowing Ghost Costume

Max likes to play pretend. When you wear your costume, think about being a silly ghost. What kinds of things would you do?

What you'll need...

- 1 45-inch square of fabric or a pillowcase
- 1 pencil
- Scissors
- 1 large paper bag
- Fabric paint or tempera paint
- Extra-tacky white crafts glue or white crafts glue
- Beads, buttons, glitter, or sequins
- 1 hat or headband

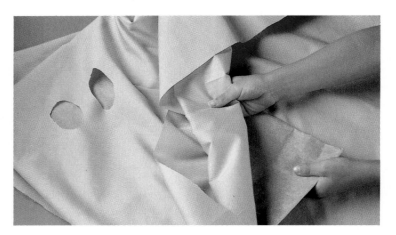

1 Put the fabric over your head. Have an adult carefully mark eyeholes with a pencil. Take the fabric off your head. Use scissors to cut out the eyeholes. (If you use a pillowcase, see page 30.) Fold the fabric into a triangle with the eyes in the front. Put a paper bag between the 2 layers of fabric (see photo).

2 Use fabric paint to draw a face on the front of the fabric (see photo). If you like, draw a design on the fabric, too.

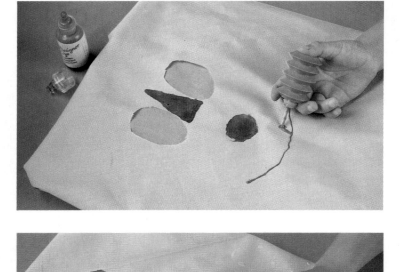

3 For other costume decorations, glue beads onto the fabric.
   To wear the costume, place the fabric over your head. Hold it in place by wearing a hat or headband.

Bake monster-size cookies from purchased cookie dough.

Spooky Cookies

Hungry little ghosts, goblins, and gremlins love to munch on these scrumptious spooks. You will, too!

What you'll need...

- 1 table knife
- One 20-ounce roll refrigerated chocolate chip or sugar cookie dough
- 2 baking sheets
- 1 metal spatula
- Wire cooling rack
- One 16-ounce can vanilla frosting
- Assorted candy
- Cookie Makeup (see tip on page 15)

1 With adult help, preheat the oven to 350°. Using the table knife, cut the roll of cookie dough crosswise into 6 equal pieces. Place 1 piece of dough on a baking sheet. Pat the dough into a 4- to 5-inch circle (see photo). Repeat with the remaining 5 pieces of dough, spacing each circle about 3 inches apart.

2 Bake the cookies for 10 to 12 minutes or till the cookies are golden brown. Cool for 2 minutes on the baking sheet. Use the metal spatula to transfer the cookies to the wire cooling rack (see photo). Cool the cookies completely.

3 Use the table knife to spread the frosting on the cooled cookies. Then, decorate each cookie any way you like with Cookie Makeup (see photo).

Cookie Makeup

For the eyes, nose, and mouth, use hard candies, shoestring licorice, candy-coated fruit-flavored pieces, or chocolate pieces. Or, draw a face with decorating gel that comes in a tube.

To brighten the faces of your cookies, stir food coloring into the vanilla frosting before spreading it.

BOO!

Form cheesecloth into a decoration for indoors or out.

Flying Ghost

Ghosts and goblins fly in the night.
Watch for them when the moon is bright.
But remember, everyone, and beware.
Ghosts and goblins will give you a scare!

What you'll need...

- 1 small bowl
- ¼ cup white crafts glue
- Two 16-inch squares of cheesecloth (2 thicknesses each)
- String
- Waxed paper
- Marker or crayon

1 In a small bowl stir together the glue and ¾ cup *water*. Lay 1 piece of cheesecloth flat. For the head, wad the other piece of cheesecloth into a ball. Put it in the middle of the square. Bring 1 corner of the square over the head to the opposite corner, making a triangle (see photo).

2 Gather the cheesecloth at the bottom of the head. With adult help, use a piece of string to tie the cheesecloth tightly below the head (see photo).

Dip the cheesecloth into the glue mixture so it's wet all over. Squeeze any extra glue mixture out of the cheesecloth and back into the bowl.

3 Reshape the ghost's body into a triangle (see photo). Pin it to a bulletin board covered with waxed paper. Or, lay the ghost on a piece of waxed paper. Let the ghost dry completely.

If you like, use a marker to draw a face on the ghost. Use the string tied below the ghost's head to hang it up for a decoration.

Travel through unknown territory in an a-maze-ing adventure.

Mysterious Monsters

Max and his friend, Bigfoot, are looking for the Abominable Snowman.
Help them follow the path to the snowman's cave.

BRIDGE IS OUT

Did you know...

● Some people believe there is a creature called Bigfoot. Stories also have been told about the Abominable Snowman. But no one has ever been able to prove these creatures are real.

● Stories say Bigfoot is much taller than most people. It is said he looks like an ape, but walks on 2 feet like you do. He lives in the woods in the mountains.

● The Abominable Snowman is said to be a white furry beast that looks like Bigfoot. He's called a snowman because he lives in the snowy mountains.

Cover the beast's body with soap flakes whipped with water.

The Abominable Snowman

Do you like snow? Max does. And, he really likes to build this kind of snowman because it never melts!

What you'll need...

- Tape
- Waxed paper
- 2 small twigs
- Snowman Body (see page 31)
- 1 jumbo craft stick or table knife
- Soapy Snow (see page 31)
- 2 buttons
- Scissors
- Construction paper
- Pins or tape

1 Tape a piece of waxed paper to your work surface. For arms, push the twigs into the Snowman Body. Use the jumbo craft stick to spread the Soapy Snow all over the Snowman Body except for the bottom (see photo).

If the Soapy Snow begins to harden while you work, stir in a few drops of water.

2 For the eyes, press the buttons into the wet Soapy Snow (see photo). Let your snowman dry completely.

Cut 2 feet out of the construction paper. Pin them to the bottom of the snowman (see photo at right).

Step into some homemade clay to make a big foot.

Bigfoot

Max has found some very LARGE footprints in the forest. He thinks they might have been made by Bigfoot. Would you like to make your footprints out of clay?

What you'll need...

- Waxed paper
- Homemade Clay (see page 32)
- Paint, markers, or crayons

1 Tape a piece of waxed paper to your work surface. Pat some of the Homemade Clay into an oval just a little larger than your foot (see photo).

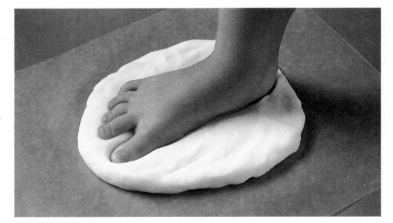

2 To make a footprint, gently step into the clay with a bare foot. For a really BIG footprint, have an adult step in the clay. Let the clay footprint dry completely. (See directions on page 32.)

3 If you like, decorate the footprint with paint.

Sea Monsters

Find the pairs of sea monsters that look the same.

Yow! Max's raft is on top of a sea monster! Luckily, this is a friendly one out with her family. Now, look closely at the little monsters. There are 4 sets of twins. Can you point to them?

24

Did you know...

● The Loch Ness Monster, nicknamed Nessie, is another much-talked-about creature like Bigfoot. The monster got its name because it supposedly lives in a lake in Scotland called Loch Ness.
● Some scientists think Nessie may be related to a dinosaurlike reptile that lived in the area many, many years ago. The creature is said to have flippers, 1 or 2 humps, and a long, thin neck.
● Many divers have searched the dark waters of the lake, but no one has proven that there really is a Loch Ness Monster.

Egg carton cups become the sea creature's bumps.

Silly Sea Serpent

If you saw a sea serpent, what do you think it would look like? How big would it be? What would it eat? Where would it live? Would you keep one in your bathtub?

What you'll need...

- Serpent Body (see page 32)
- Pencil
- String or yarn
- Scissors
- Construction paper
- White crafts glue or tape
- Serpent Head (see page 32)

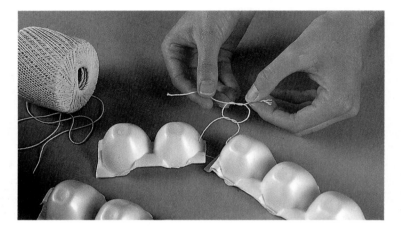

1 To join the Serpent Body sections, with adult help, use a pencil to poke a hole in one end of 2 body sections. Thread a piece of string through the hole in one section. Then thread it through the hole in the other section. Tie a knot in the string (see photo). Repeat this until you have as many body sections tied together as you want.

2 Cut eyes and a tongue out of construction paper. Glue them onto the Serpent Head (see photo).

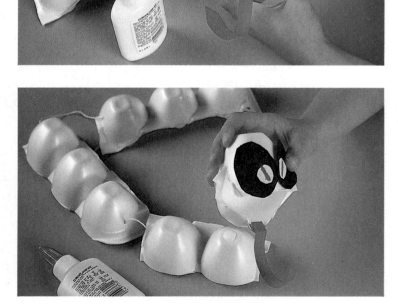

3 Glue the Serpent Head onto one of the Serpent Body sections (see photo).

If you like, use the leftover parts of the egg carton to give your monster spikes, a tail, or fins.

Let the serpent dry completely before putting it in water.

Swimming Allowed

Sea serpents are swell swimmers. So, fill a swimming pool, sink, or bathtub with some water. Then let your Silly Sea Serpent go for a swim.

Serve this home-baked treat for breakfast or a snack.

Giant Sea Snails

You won't really find giant snails in the sea, but some extra-large cinnamon snails might find their way into your tummy!

What you'll need...

- 1 pie plate
- 1 spoon
- ¼ cup finely chopped nuts
- 3 tablespoons sugar
- ½ teaspoon ground cinnamon
- 1 package (8) refrigerated breadsticks
- Waxed paper
- Shortening or nonstick spray coating
- 1 large baking sheet

1 In the pie plate stir together the nuts, sugar, and cinnamon. Remove 2 rolled-up breadsticks from the package. Place on waxed paper. Unroll 1 of the breadsticks. Press one end onto the end of the rolled-up breadstick (see photo). Wrap the unrolled breadstick around the rolled-up breadstick. Repeat with the remaining breadsticks.

2 For the head, take the free end of the breadstick and roll it a little in the other direction (see photo).

If you like, make smaller snails using 1 breadstick for each snail.

3 Put the snail in the pie plate. Flatten the snail with your hand (see photo). Remove the snail from the pie plate. Place the snail, sugared side up, on a greased baking sheet. Repeat with the remaining snails. With adult help, bake in a 375° oven about 15 minutes or till golden. Serve warm or cool. Makes 4.

Kooky Creatures

See pages 4 and 5

Children usually love to tell jokes. For a "howling" good time, share these fun monster jokes with them.

Which days of the week do monsters like best?

*Moan*days, *Tombs*days, and *Fright*days.

What game do monsters most like to play?

Hide-and-*Shriek*.

● Reading suggestion:
The Monster Riddle Book
by Jane Sarnoff and
Reynold Ruffins

Ugfuzz

See pages 6 and 7

Our kid-testers had a great time decorating this fuzzy character—and the uglier the better! They were especially intrigued with the idea of adding teeth to its face.

We have learned that younger children have trouble visualizing where to put the face on their projects. To help them get started, offer suggestions such as giving the monster 1 or 2 eyes. Or, perhaps the eyes could go on the side or back of the head instead of the front.

The Blob

See pages 8 and 9

Your children may want to use this fun painting technique to make greeting cards. They can make patterns by tracing the shape of a cookie cutter on a

piece of paper and cutting it out. Paint the pattern as directed on page 8.

Mostly Ghosts

See pages 10 and 11

While adults find illustrated ghosts and monsters funny or cute, children may be frightened of these imaginary creatures. By reading books to your children that render the monster friendly, you may help alleviate their fears.

● Reading suggestions:
There's a Nightmare in My Closet
by Mercer Mayer
Where the Wild Things Are
by Maurice Sendak

Glowing Ghost Costume

See pages 12 and 13

For a pillowcase costume, cut a slit about halfway up the center of the back. Cut a slit on each side of the pillowcase for the armholes. Then continue with the directions on page 12.

Spooky Cookies

See pages 14 and 15

Serve this warm and colorful cider with your cookies.

Raspberry Cider

10 cups apple cider or apple juice
1 12-ounce package frozen red raspberries (lightly sweetened)
5 inches stick cinnamon

● In a large saucepan combine apple cider, raspberries, and cinnamon. Bring to boiling; reduce heat. Cover; simmer 10 minutes. Remove from heat.
● Strain the raspberries and cinnamon from cider mixture through 100 percent cotton cheesecloth.
● If desired, cover and chill mixture. Serve cold or reheat till warm. Makes 16 servings.

Flying Ghost

See pages 16 and 17

For Halloween, create a spooky atmosphere outdoors by filling your trees with Flying Ghosts. Either hang the ghosts to dry over a small tree branch, or use string to hang dry ones.

A Monster Party

What do monsters, costumes, and food all have in common? You find them at a Halloween party. But what about a little monster mania other times of the year? Plan such a party for your children and their friends using some of these fun and inexpensive ideas.

Invitations: Get your children involved in the planning by having them create their own invitations using The Blob project on pages 8 and 30. To save on extra postage, start with paper that will fit into a regular envelope. Be sure to include the theme, date, time, place, and anything special the child should bring, such as a costume or birthday gift.

Decorations: Add some haunted to your house with the Flying Ghost project (page 16) or the Glowing Ghost Costume (page 12). To use the costume, blow up a balloon for the head and drape the costume over the balloon, tying a string around the neck. Place the spooks near the front door to greet guests.

Weave spiderwebs by pulling polyester fiberfill very thin. Drape it over furniture and picture frames. For spiders, use a nut cup or egg carton cup for bodies. Use the tip of a pencil to poke holes around the bottom edge of the cup. Insert pipe cleaners or twist-ties into the holes for legs.

Party Activities: Instead of playing lots of games, have the children make projects like Ugfuzz (page 6) or the Silly Sea Serpent (page 26). Set up a table with the supplies they'll need, including some especially fun craft items such as glitter, paint, wiggle eyes, colored cotton balls, beads, and fabric trims such as rick rack or lace.

Also, consider Spooky Cookies (page 14) as a party activity. Prepare the cookies ahead except for decorating. Then turn the kids loose to "face paint" their cookie. Serve the cookies as their treat with Raspberry Cider (page 30) or wrap up the cookie for them to take home.

Mysterious Monsters

See pages 18 and 19

Track down the tales of Bigfoot and the Abominable Snowman at your library. You'll find both fiction and nonfiction books to intrigue readers of all ages.
● Reading suggestions:
The Mystery of the Giant Footprints
by Fernando Krahn
Monster Tracks?
by A. Delaney

The Abominable Snowman

See pages 20 and 21

When you select the size of the snowman's body, remember most young children won't have the patience to completely cover it with Soapy Snow. So it's probably a good idea to give them a petite snowman.

Snowman Body: For the snowman shown in the photographs on page 20, use two or three 2½- to 3-inch plastic-foam balls. Cut the bottom off one of the balls so the body will stand up. Push a toothpick *halfway* into the top of one ball. Then push the rest of the toothpick into a second ball. Repeat these steps to add a third ball. Or, use a small plastic container for the body. Cut a hole in each side to push the arms through.

Soapy Snow

1¼ cups soap flakes (such as Ivory Snow)
⅔ cup water

● In a mixer bowl combine the soap flakes and water. Beat with an electric mixer on high speed till fluffy. Makes about 1¾ cups snow.

Bigfoot

See pages 22 and 23

Use this clay for Christmas ornaments, too. Roll the clay about ¼ inch thick. Cut out shapes with your favorite cookie cutters. Use a straw to

poke a hole at the top of the shape. When dry, thread a ribbon through the hole and hang the ornaments on a tree.

Homemade Clay
● In a large saucepan combine 1 cup *cornstarch* and one 1-pound box *baking soda*. Stir in 1½ cups *water*. Cook and stir over low heat till mixture thickens and forms a ball.
● Remove from heat. Turn clay out onto a surface dusted lightly with cornstarch. When cool enough to handle, knead the clay till smooth.
● Cover clay; cool completely. Use to make footprints. (If desired, tightly wrap clay and refrigerate up to 2 weeks. When ready to use, knead to soften.)
● To dry, place footprints on a baking sheet. Bake in a 300° oven 30 minutes. Shut off the oven; leave baking sheet in oven 1 hour more. If the clay is still not dry, place the footprint on a wire rack and air-dry it.
● You can air-dry the clay instead of using the oven. It will take several days for thicker pieces of clay. Thinner pieces, such as the Christmas ornaments, will dry overnight.

Sea Monsters

See pages 24 and 25

When your children have sorted out the pairs of sea monsters, try a new game.

Put pairs of everyday objects such as spools, silverware, socks, and buttons in a bag or box. Dump everything out on the floor or table and ask your children to match the ones that look alike.

Playing these "games" helps children learn to sort similar objects into sets and to know how and why they belong together. This is a basic skill necessary for language, logical thought, and number.

Sea Serpent

See pages 26 and 27

A good adhesive to use on plastic foam is extra-tacky white crafts glue. It is widely available at fabric and crafts stores.
Serpent Body: Remove the lid and flap from a plastic-foam egg carton. Cut the egg cups into 4 sections with 3 cups in each section. Use 2 or 3 sections for the body.

Serpent Head: Use 2 single egg cups. Place 1 egg cup upright. Invert the other egg cup and glue or tape to the top of the first cup. Or, use 1 egg cup.

To make the large blue serpent on page 27, cut 2 egg cups crosswise off one end of the egg carton for the head. Use the remaining part of the egg carton for the body.
● Reading suggestions:
Cyrus the Unsinkable Sea Serpent
  by Bill Peet
The Mysterious Tadpole
  by Steven Kellogg

Giant Sea Snails

See pages 28 and 29

Make learning fun by using the ingredients for Giant Sea Snails to help your children recognize letters and numbers. Begin by shaping each breadstick into a letter or number on a greased baking sheet. Sprinkle the sugar mixture over the breadstick with a spoon. Bake in a 375° oven for 10 to 12 minutes or till golden.

BETTER HOMES AND GARDENS® BOOKS
Editor: Gerald M. Knox   Art Director: Ernest Shelton   Managing Editor: David A. Kirchner
Family Life Editor: Sharyl Heiken

CREEPY MONSTERS
Editors: Jennifer Darling and Sandra Granseth   Graphic Designers: Harjis Priekulis and Linda Vermie
Project Manager: Jennifer Speer Ramundt
Contributing Illustrator: Buck Jones   Contributing Photographer: Scott Little

Have BETTER HOMES AND GARDENS® magazine delivered to your door.
For information write to: ROBERT AUSTIN, P.O. BOX 4536, DES MOINES, IA 50336